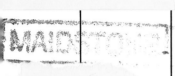

Steven Gerrard

by

Andy Croft

Illustrated by Dylan Gibson

First published in 2011 in Great Britain by
Barrington Stoke Ltd
18 Walker St, Edinburgh, EH3 7LP

www.barringtonstoke.co.uk

ISBN: 978-1-84299-485-6

Printed in Great Britain by Bell & Bain Ltd

From the Author

You don't have to be a Liverpool fan to like Liverpool. They are one of the great English football clubs. A great club with a great history.

I have been to most grounds in the Premiership. Old Trafford is bigger. St James's Park is noisier. The Emirates is more expensive. But Anfield is special. It is full of ghosts. You can feel the history. The players and the managers. The fans who died at Heysel and Hillsborough.

I'm not a Liverpool fan. But I am a fan of Stevie G. Lots of great players have played for Liverpool. Ian Rush, Kenny Dalglish, Roger Hunt, John Barnes and Robbie Fowler. They made history. Like Steven Gerrard. Here's his story.

For Dave, a loyal Red

Contents

1   You'll Never Walk Alone   1

2   Liverpool Red   6

3   This is Anfield   13

4   Istanbul   24

5   King of the Kop   31

6   Three Lions on the Shirt   37

7   Stevie G   49

Chapter 1

You'll Never Walk Alone

It's FA Cup semi-final day, 15th of April 1989. Liverpool are playing Notts Forest at Hillsborough in Sheffield. Local rivals Everton are playing Norwich in the other semi-final. Everyone on Merseyside wants Liverpool and Everton to meet in the final.

Steven Gerrard is eight years old. He's already football mad. He's a big Liverpool fan. His favourite player is Liverpool captain Ronnie Whelan. Steven's 10-year-old cousin Jon-Paul has gone to watch the game at Hillsborough. But Steven is at home in Liverpool, listening to the game on the radio. He is really excited. With players like John Barnes, Ian Rush, Alan Hansen, John Aldridge and Steve McMahon, the Reds should win.

Hillsborough is packed. The game kicks off. Liverpool begin to attack. Peter Beardsley hits the Forest post. But then the

2

ref blows his whistle. What for? He's stopping the game. After only six minutes. What's going on? Some fans are climbing onto the pitch. There's a problem in one of the stands. But it's not a fight. There is a crush in the Leppings Lane end. There are too many fans in the ground. Some of them are trying to get out. Steven's dad turns on the TV news. They can't believe it. There are bodies all over the pitch. Some of them are lying very still ...

It is the worst accident in British football history. Nearly 800 fans have been hurt.

Ninety-six Liverpool fans are dead. One of the fans who will never come home is Steven's cousin Jon-Paul.

Steven can't believe it. He is shocked, upset and angry. But that day he makes up his mind to become a top footballer. In memory of his cousin, Jon-Paul. "The Hillsborough disaster," he says, "drove me on to become the player I am today."

This is the story of the eight-year-old Liverpool fan who grew up to become one of their all-time greatest players.

Chapter 2

Liverpool Red

Steven Gerrard was born in Liverpool on the 30th of May 1980. He lived with his dad Paul, his mum Julie and his older brother Paul at number 10, Ironside Road, on the Bluebell Estate.

Lots of footballers have grown up in that part of the city – Joey Barton (Newcastle), Peter Reid (Man City), Craig Hignett (Middlesbrough), Steve McMahon (Liverpool) and David Nugent (Burnley). Steven and his friends played football all the time, mostly on the road and on the local fields.

The Gerrard family were football mad. Steven's dad used to coach a boys' team. His cousin Anthony plays for Cardiff City. His uncle Les used to take him to Goodison Park. He wanted him to support Everton, not Liverpool. But his dad was a Liverpool fan.

He took Steven to Anfield. Steven loved it.
They were standing at the Kop end in 1989
when Michael Thomas won the title for
Arsenal with a goal in the last minute of the
last match of the season.

Steven went to St Michael's Primary
School and Cardinal Heenan RC High School.
He was always small for his age, but he still
played for the school teams. He once scored
100 goals in a season! His best subject –
apart from football – was English. He liked
writing stories. He once wrote a story about
playing in the World Cup final.

When he was nine he started playing for Whiston Juniors. Scouts from Liverpool soon heard about the wonder-kid from Ironside Road. They asked him to join other young players with talent at the club's Centre of Excellence. It was like a dream come true. But there are lots of nine-year-olds with talent. Not many become top players. It takes a really special kid to make it all the way to the top.

Who could have guessed that this skinny little nine-year-old would one day captain Liverpool?

They used to train twice a week after school. The coach was the famous Steve Heighway. Michael Owen (now at Man United) and Jason Koumas (now at Wigan) were also there. Steven loved it.

But a few months later he stabbed his toe on a rusty garden fork. The doctors wanted to cut his toe off. Maybe even his right foot. Steven's dad rang Anfield. Steve Heighway drove round to the hospital and begged them not to cut off his foot. In the end they agreed. Steven Gerrard's career was saved.

By the time Steven was 16, he had offers to join Crystal Palace, Everton, West Ham, Man City and Man United. Spurs offered two million pounds for him after he played against them in an under-17s game. But there was only one club for Steven Gerrard. "Cut me," he says, "and I bleed Liverpool red."

Chapter 3

This is Anfield

Steven left school in 1996 when he was 16. He joined the Liverpool Youth Academy. He earned just £50 a week. Michael Owen and Jamie Carragher were there at the same time.

They had to train hard and work hard. It wasn't all football. They had to look after the first team players' boots and kit. They had to collect signed shirts, balls and photos for the fans. Sometimes they even had to clean the changing rooms. But Steven didn't mind. He loved it.

At first he was a bit frightened of the first team stars like Robbie Fowler, John Barnes and Jamie Redknapp. But they soon became mates. And sometimes the young lads were allowed to train with the first team players.

When Steven was 17 the club gave him a three year contract. By now he was earning £700 a week! Everyone could see that the young Steven Gerrard was going to be a great player. He was strong, brave and fast. He could run, pass and head the ball. He could read the game. He had a great shot. And he loved tackling. "I was put on this earth to steam into tackles," he said. He loved winning. And he *hated* losing.

In 1998 Gérard Houlier became manager of Liverpool. He wanted to make Liverpool great again. He started buying all the best players. He needed a hard-tackling mid-field

player. But he didn't need to buy anyone.

Steven Gerrard was already at Anfield,

playing in the Reserves.

In November 1998 he was included in the

first team squad against Celta Vigo in the

UEFA Cup. He was only 18. He was terrified.

And excited. He couldn't believe it was real.

Awesome.

The next week he came on as sub against

Blackburn. Liverpool won 2-0. On the 4th of

December 1998 he was in the starting line-up

against Spurs. This was the moment he had been waiting for all his life. To play for the club he had supported since he was a boy. He was so excited he couldn't sleep the night before the game.

Steven Gerrard played 13 games for Liverpool in his first season. The next year he played 31 games. He also scored his first goal for the club, against Sheff Wed, running past three defenders to blast the ball home.

In those days he played with the number 28 on his shirt. He also played all over the

pitch – left-back, right-back, centre-mid, right-mid. Liverpool fans couldn't agree which was his best position. Was he a box-to-box player? A defender? A winger? A defensive midfielder? An inside forward? The truth is – Steven Gerrard can play anywhere on the pitch.

Houlier began building a great team at Anfield – Babbel, Carragher, Murphy, Barmby, Berger, Fowler, Owen, Heskey and Gerrard.

In the 2000-2001 season, Steven Gerrard played 50 games for Liverpool and scored 10 goals. He scored in the 4-0 defeat of Arsenal. He scored his first goal against Everton in the 3-1 win at Goodison. His goal in the UEFA Cup final helped Liverpool beat the Spanish team Alaves 5-4.

At the end of that season Liverpool had won the FA Cup, the League Cup and the UEFA Cup. And they finished third in the league. Steven Gerrard was voted PFA Young Player of the Year.

The next year they reached the quarter-finals of the Champions League and finished second in the Premier League. In 2003 they

beat Man United in the League Cup final.

Gerrard scored. In October 2003 Houllier

made Gerrard the team captain. It was a

proud moment. To captain the club he loved.

In his first five seasons, Steven Gerrard

played 227 games for Liverpool and scored 34

goals.

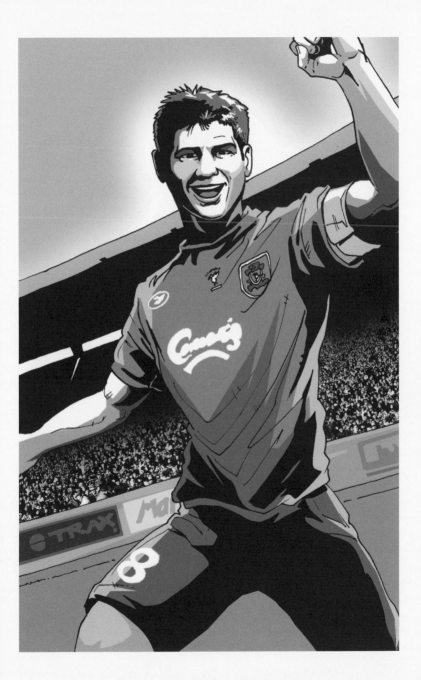

Chapter 4

Istanbul

Gérard Houlier left Liverpool in 2004.
Steven Gerrard was sorry to see him go. But
Liverpool soon had a new manager. Rafa
Benitez. He had won the Spanish League with
Valencia. Gerrard was really excited.
Benitez gave him the number 8 shirt.

At the start of the season Gerrard scored twice in the Champions League against Graz from Austria. But Liverpool were in a very hard Group. After five games they only had seven points. They had to win their last home game against the Greek Team, Olympiakos, by two goals to reach the next stage. But the Greeks took the lead. It looked like Liverpool were out. Then Pongolle scored for Liverpool. 1-1. Then Mellor put Liverpool ahead. But time was running out.

With only four minutes left, Mellor headed the ball down. Gerrard came running in and smashed it in from 22 metres out.

Fantastic goal! Liverpool were through to the

next stage. But only just.

They beat Beyer Leverkusen 6-2. They

beat Juventus 2-1. They beat Chelsea 1-0 in

the semi-final. Liverpool were in the

Champions' League final. But they had to

play AC Milan. Everyone thought that Milan

would win. They had Kaka, Crespo, Maldini,

Gattuso and Shevchenko. But Liverpool had

Steven Gerrard.

The final was in Istanbul, in Turkey on
the 25th of May, 2005. Tens of thousands of
Liverpool fans were there. But Maldini
scored for Milan in the first minute. Then
Crespo scored another. Then another.
Liverpool were losing 0-3 at half time. It
looked like it was all over. Some Liverpool
fans started leaving the ground.

But Steven Gerrard refused to give up. He
was everywhere, running, tackling, passing,
defending. In the 54th minute, John Arne
Riise crossed the ball into the Milan area.
Gerrard jumped up and sent a strong, looping

header past Dida. Goal! 1-3. Two minutes later, Vladimir Smicer scored another with a long-range shot. Goal! 2-3. Four minutes later, Gerrard burst into the box. Milan's Gattuso brought him down. Penalty! Alonso took the penalty. Dida saved it, but Alonso scored from the rebound. Goal! 3-3.

The Milan fans couldn't believe it. Nor could the Liverpool fans. Dudek made a brilliant double-save in extra time to take the game to penalties. Milan were gutted.

Liverpool won 3-2 on penalties. After the game Steven Gerrard was named Man of the Match. He was later voted UEFA Club Footballer of the Year. Five-times winners Liverpool were allowed to keep the trophy.

Chapter 5

King of the Kop

When Benitez arrived at Anfield, he told Steven Gerrard to get into the box more. He wanted him to score more goals. It worked. He scored nearly 100 goals in the next five seasons. He was Liverpool's top scorer two years running. In 2005-6 he scored 23 goals in 53 games. That's nearly one goal every two games.

He scored twice in the 2006 FA Cup final. West Ham were 2-0 up in less than half an hour. But Gerrard wouldn't give up. He crossed the ball for Cissé to pull one back. At the start of the second half, Crouch knocked the ball down to Gerrard who scored inside the box. Goal! 2-2. But West Ham scored again. 2-3. It looked like West Ham had won the Cup.

Gerrard was very tired. He had cramp. But he kept on going. In the last seconds of the game he picked up the ball in midfield and smashed it in from 30 metres out. Goal!

3-3. After extra time, Liverpool won 3-1 on penalties. Gerrard scored, of course. He was voted Man of the Match. The PFA voted him Player of the Year.

Steven Gerrard played 366 games for Liverpool in 12 seasons. He scored 80 goals. He is the only player ever to score in the FA Cup Final, the League Cup Final, the UEFA Cup Final and the Champions' League Final.

Liverpool have won more trophies than any other English club. They have won the title 18 times, the FA Cup seven times, the

League Cup seven times, the UEFA cup three times and the European Cup and Champions' League five times.

Under Benitez they have won the FA Cup. They have won the Community Shield. They have reached the Champions' League final twice, and won it once. In the league they have finished fifth, fourth, third (twice) and second. But they just can't win the Premier League. Not even with Stevie G.

At the end of 2010, Benitez left Anfield for Inter Milan. Some people thought that

Steven Gerrard might leave the club as well. But new manager Roy Hodgson persuaded him to stay. To bring the Premier League to Anfield.

Chapter 6

Three Lions on the Shirt

Steven Gerrard has come a long way. He never gives up even when things go wrong.

When he was young he never played for England schoolboys. He was too small in those days.

When he was 14 he and Michael Owen
were invited to the FA school in Lilleshall for
a trial. Owen was picked, but not Gerrard.
He was very upset. But he knew that one day
he would play for his country.

He played for England under-16s (and
scored against the Republic of Ireland). He
was captain of England under-18s (and scored
against Italy). He played for the under-21s
(and scored against Luxemburg). But he only
played four games for under-21s. He was
already needed in the first team.

In 2000 England manager Kevin Keegan
asked him to train with the senior squad. He
couldn't believe it. The FA offered to drive
him down to the training ground at Bisham.
But he was too nervous. So he drove down in
his dad's Honda.

When he reached the England hotel he hid
in his room. He was too afraid to go
downstairs and meet the first team players
like David Beckham, Tony Adams, Alan
Shearer and Sol Campbell. So the other
Liverpool players – Redknapp, Owen,
McManaman and Fowler – found him and

introduced him to the other players.
"Welcome to England," said Keegan.

A few weeks later Keegan rang him. He
wanted him to start in a friendly against
Ukraine. At first Gerrard thought it was a
joke. He thought it was one of his mates
winding him up! He was in Keegan's squad
for Euro 2000. He played in the 2-1 win over
Germany. But then he injured his leg in
training and missed the next game. Rumania
beat England 3-2. England were out.

In 2001, Gerrard scored in England's 5-1 defeat of Germany. But he hurt himself in Liverpool's last match of the season against Ipswich. He tore a muscle. He was going to miss the World Cup. The news was "like a punch in the face". He was frustrated and angry. But he couldn't do anything about it. He had to watch the 2002 World Cup at home on TV. But he made up his mind to bounce back as soon as he could. Fitter and stronger than ever.

At Euro 2004, England had a brilliant midfield – Beckham, Scholes, Lampard and

Gerrard. They started well. In the first game against France, Lampard put England 1-0 up. Zidane scored to make it 1-1. But England were in control. Then in injury time Gerrard passed it back to David James in goal. He didn't see Thierry Henry hiding behind Sol Campbell. Henry ran onto the ball and James fouled him. Penalty! Zidane scored for France to win 2-1.

Steven Gerrard was gutted. He blamed himself. But he made up for this mistake by scoring against Switzerland in the next game. He helped England beat Croatia to reach the last eight. But in the quarter-finals they drew 2-2 with Portugal and went out on penalties.

The team England took to the World Cup in 2006 was the best England team for a long time – Gerrard, Owen, Lampard, Beckham, Cole, Terry and Rooney. Gerrard played really well in the 1-0 win against Paraguay. He scored in the 2-0 win against Trinidad and Tobago. He scored again to beat Sweden. He helped England beat Equador 1-0. England were through to the quarter-finals. Again. But they had to play Portugal. Again. After

full-time the score was still 0-0. They lost on penalties. Again.

In 2010 the World Cup finals were held in South Africa. Under new manager Fabio Capello, England topped their group. Steven Gerrard played in seven of England's 10 group games. He scored three goals (three against Croatia). England won nine games and lost only one. They scored 34 goals and only let in six.

In South Africa, manager Fabio Capello made Gerrard the England captain. In the

first game, against the USA, Gerrard scored
after only four minutes. It looked like
England were on their way. But the USA
drew level and the game ended in a draw.
Although England beat Slovenia, they could
only draw against Algeria. This meant that
England had to play Germany in the next
round. As captain, Steven Gerrard tried to
lead the team by example. He was
everywhere – chasing and tackling, passing
and shooting. He did everything he could.
But England lost 4-1.

Chapter 8
Stevie G

Stevie G is used to being famous. Photographers chase him everywhere. In 2007 the Queen gave him an MBE. There is a life-size wax model of him at Madame Tussauds in London – standing next to Rooney and Beckham! When Liverpool fans were asked to vote for "100 Players Who

Shook the Kop" he came second (after Kenny Dalglish). Zinedine Zidan once said he was the best player in the world.

He helps to raise a lot of money for charity. He supports the Red Balloon appeal to build a refuge for bullied children in Liverpool. He has sold his captain's armbands to raise money for charity.

But he doesn't really like being famous. He doesn't like travelling. He doesn't like flying. And he hates being away from home. He lives near Liverpool with his wife Alex and their two little girls, Lilly-Ella and Lexie. Their names are stitched inside his boots.

Stevie G looks after himself. He doesn't smoke. He doesn't drink much. He likes Italian food, best of all pasta. He likes listening to Coldplay, Phil Collins and most dance music. His favourite books are *Mr Nice* and *Of Mice and Men*. His favourite TV comedy is *The Office*. His favourite film is *Scarface*. When he is not playing football, he watches it. When he is not watching football he likes watching England play rugby. "It's my idea of sport," he says, "big hits and bloody battles!"

Stevie G likes to battle. He is a fighter. A winner. Captain of Liverpool. Captain of England. He has won the FA Cup, the League Cup, the UEFA Cup and the Champions League. But he has never won the Premier League. It is over 20 years since Liverpool last won the title. Steven Gerrard wants to bring the Premier League back to Anfield one day. Can he do it? Is he good enough? What do you think?

Barrington Stoke would like to thank all its readers for commenting on the manuscript before publication and in particular:

Noel Bradley
Jordan Boyle
Nathan Cogley
Jake Cooney
Jennifer Cutler
Quinton Dawson
Niamh Dennehy
Glen Ellis
Sarah Ertan
Tamara Evelyn
Andrew Forde
Saad Ghani

Katie Grant
Gareth Kane
Glen Kearney
Jessica Little
Vashish Lohoharawoi
Clive Murphy
Josie O'Brien
Bethany Payne
Eva Phillips
Sophie Phillips
Darragh Somerville
Jonathan Tomlinson

Become a Consultant!

Would you like to be a consultant? Ask your parent, carer or teacher to contact us at the email address below – we'd love to hear from them! They can also find out more by visiting our website.

schools@barringtonstoke.co.uk
www.barringtonstoke.co.uk

More fab books from Barrington Stoke

**Lewis Hamilton
by
Andy Croft**

Lewis Hamilton is the first ever black Formula 1 champion. How did he get from go-karts to global fame?
Find out here!

**Sol Campbell
by
Andy Croft**

From racism to success.
From hard times to fast cars.
From school team to World Cup squad.

The true story of fame, fortune and a footballing superstar.

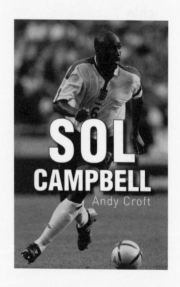

You can order these books directly from our website at
www.barringtonstoke.co.uk

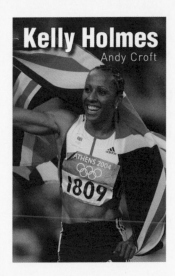
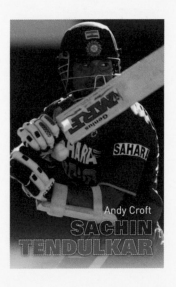